# QUOTABLE USTINOV

# QUOTABLE USTINOV

59 John Glenn Drive
Amherst, NewYork 14228-2197

Published 1995 by Prometheus Books.
This edition is published by arrangement with
Michael O'Mara Books Limited, London.

First published in Great Britain in 1995 by
Michael O'Mara Books Limited
9 Lion Yard
Tremadoc Road
London SW4 7NQ



Typeset and designed by Robert Updegraff

Library of Congress Cataloging-in-Publication Data

Ustinov, Peter
Quotable Ustinov / Peter Ustinov.
p. cm.
ISBN 1-57392-025-8 (hardback : alk. paper)
1. Ustinov, Peter--Quotations. 2. Quotations, English.
I. Title.
PR6041.S73A6 1995 95-21226
828'.91402--dc20 CIP

Printed in the United States of America on acid-free paper.

# Contents

Preface 5
Life Through the Rear-View Mirror 7
A Glimpse of God 18
Very Important People 24
Without a Drop of English Blood 36
A Nervous Little Wine 53
A Funny Way of Being Serious 56
The Weakest Voices, The Best Ideas 77
Opera 84
Eureka! 89
But a Ball Makes My Teeth Grate 98
A Form of Incontinence 110
Hearing Voices 115
Love Thy Neighbour, but Build a Wall 127
It's Dangerous to Lean out of Windows 136
School Reports 147
Changing the Subject 155
Hollywood 177
A Midwife Needs a Baby 183
Likes 189
Dislikes 191
Men, Women and Children 196

THE LARGEST
TURNOUT AT
ELECTIONS
ARE ALWAYS
WHERE THERE IS
ONLY ONE
CANDIDATE

# Preface

Quotable? I must say I am amazed that there is anything worth quoting in my extensive writings, but I must bow to those with superior knowledge, who actually succeeded in collecting sufficient quotes to justify a slender volume. Let me also admit that I read the result without much feeling of paternity, and consequently I enjoyed the result of other people's labours as though these quotes had nothing to do with me. Curiously enough, I agree with most of the quotes, and they even have a ring of familiarity. All this may have something to do with having had a long, active life, because even today I hesitate before uttering something remotely quotable, simply because I wonder if I have not said it before elsewhere. It is, of course, reprehensible to steal from others, but it is plain stupid to steal from yourself. It is also very dangerous to quote from dramatic works, since the words a dramatist places in the mouths of a serial murderer or a Nazi gauleiter are certainly not what the author would wish to have attributed to him. Quotes have to have a life of their own even out of context. They must be self-contained, and not rely on unexpressed thoughts for their effect. A diet of crumbs is hardly a square meal, but if your appetite is the opposite of hearty, and if it takes little to stimulate your own ideas on a wide variety of themes, then this book may well appeal to you. Since the evidence points to my being its father, I sincerely hope it does.

PETER USTINOV

# *Life Through the Rear-View Mirror*

## ON LIFE

Life, as John F. Kennedy remarked, is unfair, but remember: sometimes it is unfair in your favour.

## ON SUNDAYS

The best thing about Sunday is never having to get fully dressed. I often don't even get so far as putting my socks on.

### On what he learned in the army

If you want to do a thing badly, you have to work as hard at it as though you want to do it well.

### On doing the right thing

In my day there were things that were done and things that were not done and there was even a way of doing the things that were not done.

### On being a baby

I was spherical in form and everyone heaved a sigh of relief whenever I performed the exploit with my neck, since at those moments it was possible to see whether I was the right way up or not.

UNEASY GHOSTS

### On killing time

I'm only killing time, and find I'm damn bad at it.

### On his seventieth birthday

I regard every year as an achievement largely because my father told me just prior to his fiftieth birthday that he wouldn't live till seventy. Several hours before his seventieth birthday he died. It was very eerie, and it worried me a great deal last year. I was glad to round the corner past it.

### On life

Life is a marathon in which you reserve the sprint for the end.

## ON HIS PASSPORT, EXPIRING IN THE YEAR 2000

I regard it as a matter of honour not to expire before the passport.

## ON WHY HE CONTINUES PERFORMING

I keep on going because even at my age I feel slightly better after a performance than before it, and I consider it more intelligent and lucrative than jogging.

## ON LIFE

Life is imperfect and therefore it must be lived to the full.

## On clothes

I will very often go to a big-man's shop where it is a tremendous luxury to be told they've got nothing my size. I come out elated. Then I go to a normal shop and get depressed when *they* have got nothing my size. I remember my depression in America at one of those emporia where a man took my measurements and bawled out, 'Tom, we got any 54 portly?'

## On Auditioning for Nero in Quo Vadis

When the filming was delayed for a year, the new producer of the film sent him a cable saying that he thought Ustinov was a little young for the part. Ustinov sent him another cable saying that if the film was delayed another year, he would be too old for it. MGM then sent him a cable saying, 'Historical research has proved you correct.'

SIC TRANSIT

## ON LIFE

Life is too short but it would be absolutely awful if it were too long.

## On reaching seventy

When I turned seventy, I gathered all my children – four, which is not bad considering I am not a Catholic. I said to them: 'I've reached a certain age and I must, sooner or later, decide what I am going to do with my life.' There was a pause and my son said: 'Don't hurry!'

## On kids

I never had much rapport with kids – even when I was a kid.

## On Father Christmas

I have always looked on Father Christmas as a kind of reactionary symbol of comfort and affluence.

### ON WHEN HE WOULD LIKE TO DIE

At the end of a sentence.

### ON BEING FACED WITH 800 FRIENDS AND ADMIRERS AT A PARTY FOR HIS SEVENTIETH BIRTHDAY

With so many familiar faces here, it's like driving through the rear-view mirror.

### ON GETTING OLD

It was some years ago, at a big UNICEF gathering with Madame Giscard d'Estaing, whose husband was then President of France. She was accompanied by an *aide-de-camp*, who was an elderly French general, an aristocratic warrior of extreme decrepitude. He suddenly saw me and exclaimed: 'Ah, Ustinov, the hero of my youth!'

## On work

I am conscious of being engaged in a marathon rather than a sprint so that mentally I pace myself. I have got an energy bank account and I can't afford to be overdrawn.

## On regret

I have none. They are a waste of time which is becoming more and more valuable.

## On the quality of life

At my age, quality worries me less than quantity.

## On not being a politician

If I were a politician I would immediately stop being knowledgable about politics. You have to stand further away to get a view of the pictures in the gallery. That's my job.

# *A Glimpse of God*

## On religion

I am discouraged by organized religion. I love the theatre but that doesn't mean I have to have an affair with an agent to prove it.

## On death

Death is death, whether it comes in the form of a missile launched by a madman or from a source convinced of its moral ascendancy. Only the survivors see the difference and allow their prejudices to colour the hypocrisy without which all conflict quickly loses its meaning.

MONK ILLUMINATING A LETTER IN THE MIDDLE AGES

## ON RELIGION

Religion is the work of God, perfected by the Devil.

O.K FELLERS. HERE COMES ST. FRANCIS... ON THE DOWNBEAT, I WANT UNRELIEVED BIRDSONG TILL THE BELLS START

## On religion

Religion is superstition. It makes a man conscious of the alternatives.

## On death

Courage is not a requisite for the loss of life.

## On religion

Every religion is very much a reflection of a culture and a way of life. In some instances, as in the case of the fundamentalists, it purports to be an entire way of life, but in more sober societies it is content to be a condiment which gives its particular flavour to existence.

### On God

Part of the fun and mystery of life is that you don't know, but there are hints all over the place. A twinge of concience is a glimpse of God.

### On visiting the Vatican

The attitude of the Vatican was a very interesting and Jesuitical one, that 'We can't censor you outside, so what's the point of trying to censor you inside the Vatican?' Actually, it was a way of putting us on our best behaviour.

### On Christianity

I've always been interested in the fact that Rome seems to have a predestination for religious activity, churches built upon churches upon a temple of pagan ritual. In ordinary history books, it always seems the transformation to Christianity was a flash of light, a revolution. But Rome's liberal attitude to all religions is more interesting – Christianity just happened to win.

## On worship

It is the act of worship itself which is important, not what you are worshipping. A pagan worshipping a mountain or a tree is discovering the exact relative importance of himself to the universe and is putting something above himself, which is essential for the human condition.

# *Very Important People*

## On the rich and influential

Even somebody very important cuts themselves down to size when they discuss the weather.

## On heroes

I am not a hero worshipper. We admire people for their strengths but love them for their weaknesses.

### On experts

Beware of experts. The day humans blow up the world with The Bomb the last survivor will be an expert saying it can never happen.

### On Laurence Olivier

At his worst, he could have acted the parts more ably than they are usually lived.

### On George Bernard Shaw

All the characters that GBS disliked had very strong arguments.

OUI
"THE PRINCE SPOKE IN FLUENT, IF SLIGHTLY ACCENTED, FRENCH", THE TIMES

## On being invested with a knighthood

I have been a little wary of the ceremony ever since receiving a printed card with the instruction: delete whichever is inapplicable: I can kneel / I can not kneel. There was nothing for those who could kneel but not get up.

## On being king for a day

If I were king for a day, I would wait for tomorrow before putting over reforms.

## On Shakespeare

Shakespeare was a careless dramatist, even though he was probably the least careless dramatist of his age, and the reason for his persistence, his glorious survival, is not only because he was a poet of genius but because he was conscious of the possibilities of acting, and wrote for actors, not pedants.

## On Marlon Brando appearing in *The Egyptian*

Of course, by now, Marlon Brando was no longer part of the cast. He had taken one look at the final script, and become victim of a rare illness, from which he made a miraculous recovery once shooting had begun on his replacement.

## On avant-garde playwrights and actors

The *avant-garde* are rushing up a cul-de-sac and by the time they get back to the main road everyone will have gone past them.

## On pompous film directors

Most producers tend to read things before they decide whether they are going to do them. It's only the very, very important ones who say: 'I'm going to shoot *The Phone Book* next autumn,' having made the decision in all majesty.

## On Alfred Hitchcock's alleged remark that actors should be treated like animals

Everybody's opinions are formed by their own talent.

## ON DOING NOTHING IN THE FILM *ONE OF OUR AIRCRAFT IS MISSING*

Hugh Williams . . . watched me rehearse my Dutch priest with an acuity which made me singularly uncomfortable. Eventually, he came up to me and asked, with commendable politeness, 'Excuse me, young man, what exactly are you going to do in this scene?'
'I don't really know, Mr Williams,' I replied, and added hopefully, 'I thought I'd do nothing.'
A trace of hardness entered his eyes and voice. 'Oh no you don't,' he said. '*I'm* doing nothing.'

## ON ORSON WELLES

Orson is too dominant to be dominated by Shakespeare, and Shakespeare too elusive to be subjugated by anyone. But Orson's reverence for what was beautiful and noble, his curiosity before anything worthy of investigation, were unalloyed. He vacillated between the quick reactions of a journalist and the more contemplative approach of a thinker, but above all he was a creator.

## ON APPEARING ON TELEVISION

The only people who haven't appeared on television are those that are too busy watching it.

## ON POLITICIANS APPEARING ON TELEVISION

Politicians are not taught to put themselves over on television. The more charming they are the less you believe. I remember once watching Harold Macmillan on the box. He kept looking at the camera as though it were a cobra. He was appealing to the nation for calm and his face was frozen with terror.

## ON HIS GRANDDAUGHTER

She doesn't call me Grandpapa, she calls me Grospapa.

## ON POLITICIANS

By their very existence, politicians are unpopular the world over. They are seen as devious because of their baggage of confidences, and boring because they have little to say, and fail to say it well. Their only freedom is to criticize their opponents to the accompaniment of a public yawn.

## ON AUDREY HEPBURN

Statistics tell us that Audrey died young. What no statistics can show is that Audrey would have died young at any age.

## On John Gielgud

I once saw him on a local late-night television interview in Saint Louis, Missouri. He was busy playing *The Ages of Man,* his one-man show, in half a ball-park, and now he was being interviewed by a long-winded intellectual.

'One final question,' the interviewer said. 'Sir . . . Sir Gielgud . . . did you . . . oh, you must have had . . . we all did . . . at the start of your very wonderful . . . very wonderful and very meaningful . . . let me put it this way . . . did you have someone . . . a man . . . or . . . or indeed, a woman . . . at whom you could now point a finger and say . . . Yes! . . . This person helped me when I . . .'

By now John understood what was being asked of him, and he prepared to answer, disguising his dislike of all that is pretentious by a perfect courtesy.

'Yes, I think there was somebody who taught me a great deal at my dramatic school, and I certainly am grateful to him for all his kindness and consideration towards me. His name was Claude Rains.'

And then, as an afterthought, he added, 'I don't know what happened to him. I think he failed and went to America.'

## On Alec Guinness

Guinness is a mysterious, demure and secretive man. At one time he was obsessed with the desire to play Hitler and was devastated to hear Dustin Hoffman was up for the part. He dressed himself in Nazi uniform, hired a cameraman, drove to Little Venice and began an impromptu screen test. Nobody paid him the least bit of notice except a policeman who came up and said, 'Excuse me sir, is that your car ...?'

## On Pavarotti on the tennis court

You were very difficult to pass at the net with or without a racket.

## On Pavarotti's voice

You are like someone who has swallowed a Stradivarius.

## On Charles Laughton

He was always hovering around waiting to be offended. We'd see him floating in his own pool and it was just the reverse of an iceberg - ninety per cent of him was visible.

# *Without a Drop of English Blood*

## On the German sense of humour

I hate to disappoint anyone who happens to think that Germans don't have a sense of the ridiculous. They do, yet they are a reflective cultured nation, not impatient for laughter like the British.

## On Australia

I enjoy Australia a great deal. It is like America without the complexes. Australians are able to talk about anything.

## On Japan

It is disconcerting to be naked in a Japanese bath and be massaged by a young girl who has picked up a few English phrases, and remarks, as she is walking up and down your spine: 'Changeable weather we're having lately!'

## On Russia

For a country which has condemned the cult of personality, Russia is curiously paradoxical. It is practically the only nation which names ships, streets, auto factories and even whole towns after living people. That's why it has to change the names of its streets, ships and cities so often.

## On Switzerland

The Swiss are the only nation where the shop-keepers over-cut each other.

THEN & NOW

## On the French

There's nothing older than a young Frenchman. They are all prematurely old in spirit.

## On France

If I make a mistake in French everybody knows it. If I make one in English they think it's probably deliberate.

## On Russia

One of the few things about Russia worth encouraging is press interviewing. There they submit an English translation of the article about you for your signature and approval and then pay you thirty-seven roubles and fourteen kopecks for it. A minor snag is that you have to spend the money in Russia – and there's a limit to the number of fur hats a man needs.

## On the French

The French and the British are such good enemies that they can't resist being friends.

## On contracts

An English contract is untranslatable into French if it is unskilful, or, if it is skilful, it is open to two or three translations, all of them accurate and all of them different.

## On the dangers of dual nationality in times of war

By German law I suppose I'm still German because my father was until he became British. I had a German passport till 1936, when I gave it up. It would have been tricky for me if I had been captured in the war by the Germans. They would not only have shot me for being a traitor but also clapped me in jail for failing to report with my call-up group.

### On nationalism

Absolutely prehistoric.

### On his roots

Someone asked where my roots were and I said, I hope in civilized behaviour.

### On Italy

Only a person with a stony heart could avoid having a soft spot in it for Italy. It always riled Mussolini, a man with a very Italian gift for self-delusion, that his country produced waiters and maitre d's in such profusion and of such universally accepted excellence.

### On Europeans

To arrive at the truth, the Germans add, the French subtract and the English change the subject.

### On airport trolleys

There has been a great increase in the number of trolleys worldwide, which is a blessing, even if some airports, notably a few in Germany and Belgium, make you pay for them in local change.

### On holidays

Holidays are a vital reminder of what man was before human ingenuity invaded his sanctuary with endless distractions.

## On the French language

French is a poor language because of its precision. English is a vague language and a rich language because of its vagueness. You notice it with actors. If you watch a play by Tennessee Williams in French the actors can't cope with people who have no structure in the way they talk. Even a French taxi driver talks like an academician.

## On Parisian women

Paris women are truly elegant. They are not terrified when they hit thirty.

MITTERAND KEEPING HIS OWN COUNSEL

## On Rome

Rome, like so many human manifestations which appear monolithic is, in fact, a glorious city with a more than chequered history. It has known defeat, occupation, humiliation and desecration as well as triumph. Enough, at least, to earn it the description of Eternal.

## On the French, and the meaning of 'les vacances'

There is no people which so clearly divides the working year from 'les vacances', the vacations. It seems as though everyone lays down their tools virtually on the same day, in order to transfer the overcrowding of the cities on to the coastline. Then, on another prescribed day, they all evacuate the coastline and reoccupy the cities, travelling like plagues of locusts; very slow locusts with generally bad tempers.

## On the English

I have always thought that the English were really an extremely romantic, violent and tempestuous nation by nature.

## On national character

I am sure the Russian character is formed by those enormous distances. In Russia you find yourself with a man you have never seen before and he's telling you the story of his divorce and his mother's suicide within two minutes, because they are desperate to give you the impression that the country is smaller than it is. In England, when eight people sit in a railway carriage, they pretend not to see each other in order to give the impression that the country is really much bigger than it is.

## On language

I don't want there to be a universal language. I think the tower of Babel was a very good thing. If we all understood each other without the need for interpreters we would have destroyed each other a long time ago. I think that very often grave crises have been avoided by the fact that the translator either deliberately or by accident mistranslated what statesmen said to each other.

## On descent

Without a drop of English blood I was born an Englishman.

## On visiting the Soviet Union before glasnost

A friend of mine in Paris, a photographer of Russian origin, decided to visit his unknown homeland. His mother threw up her hands in distress but since she could not prevent her son from going she asked him to bring back a little soil from the ancestral town of Tver so she could scatter it on her husband's grave in Paris. The son made the icy, winter journey and descended from the train at Tver. To dig up the earth, he had to scrape away the snow first. As he was doing this, he heard the pounding of heavy feet approaching. His collar was seized by a guard with a machine-gun who demanded, ominously, why my friend was taking liberties with state property. When the reason for the digging was explained, the guard thrust his machine-gun into my friend's hands, fell to his knees in the snow and vigorously attacked the earth. He wrapped the soil carefully in some newspaper and tied it nice and tight. Then he briskly exchanged his parcel for his gun and continued his stern stewardship of the Soviet present, while my friend returned to Paris with the soil of Holy Russia wrapped in a copy of *Izvestiya*. . . Reverence, affection, sentiment: are these not among the finest qualities of humanity? I have found that the Russians have extraordinary feeling for their land and their past.

## On the USA

The States are richer than other countries in many things. Because of their unending expanses and huge horizons and the relative absence of disillusionment in their history, they are richer in dreams as well. Unfortunately, the balance of nature is paid for by a growing potential for nightmares.

## On Franco dying

Rousing momentarily from his coma, the Spanish dictator asked querulously: 'What is that noise outside the Palace?' 'It is the Spanish people,' replied a tearful aide. 'They have come to say goodbye.' 'Ah,' nodded Franco. Then, after a pause, he added, 'Where are they going?'

## ON PLAYING NATIONAL ANTHEMS, WHEN ATHLETES WIN THE OLYMPIC GAMES

Human nature being what it is, it is far too early to eliminate the playing of national anthems from the ceremonies of the podium. The moved faces of some gold-medalists are eloquent testimony to their motivation and the consummation of their ambitions. After all, this is the civilized substitute for war, appealing to exactly the same instincts as those which lingered in the heart of the Neanderthal man, and which haunt us to this day. The difference being that there the damage is confined to broken legs, broken ankles, broken arms, hamstrings, ligaments and even broken spirits, but only in the rarest misfortunes to death. In every sense the Olympics are a tremendous advance on war, and compared to the firebrand patriots of the past, the TV commentators are, on reflection, merely amusing.

## On travel

I enjoy getting there but travel has become a nightmare because it has become so prolonged. You spend hours in the airport with luggage trolleys which look like abandoned prototypes for Bleriot's aircraft.

# A Nervous Little Wine

## On the wine from his own vineyard in Switzerland

The sort we grow ourselves is a nervous little white wine, best for drinking at events like baptisms, weddings and divorces.

## On ripe Camembert

I know of nobody who did not wince when they first tried a ripe Camembert. Then it becomes an acquired taste. And from there it can become an addiction. Like most things in life.

### On investing in a film

In the inexplicable film world cowardice increases in relation to the amount of money invested.

### On fish

When I was small, I would refuse to drink water when I ate fish because I thought the fish would reconstitute itself in my stomach.

### On genes

'The devils,' she hissed, 'they didn't give me a chance. They fell in love with each other's noses. They fell in love with themselves. A child of theirs didn't have a hope in hell! It had to have that nose!'

*A Nose by Any Other Name*

# *A Funny Way of Being Serious*

## On Audiences

I have always found that audiences near the sea tend to be better than those very far inland.

## On Nero

Mervyn LeRoy, the director of *Quo Vadis*, gave me this gem of advice on how to play the Emperor Nero: 'The way I sees Nero, this is the kinda guy who plays with himself nights.'

## On the standard of acting

Technically, I think music and theatre have improved enormously. I would say the standard of acting is perilously high – to the extent that if I conduct auditions and get a really bad actor, I keep him a little longer than necessary because it is so refreshing!

## On being funny

When I try to be funny, nothing happens.

## On living the theatre

I have a dread of people who say the theatre is their life. They end up in a home where they can't relax comfortably, and where they are expecting the curtain to go up any moment, and they have forgotten their lines.

## ON ACTING

I have never understood by what mysterious means an actor retains long and intricate texts. Having played King Lear twice and Peer Gynt on TV, I still don't understand the process of that extraordinary computer lodged in our heads. Unlike in modern motorcars, we cannot turn a key and be reassured by a mass of little logos that everything is working perfectly or that the back off-side door is slightly ajar. As we sit in the dressing-room five minutes before curtain rise with nothing to listen to but that dreadful babble of the audience through the intercom, like the noise of a gigantic cocktail party, there is absolutely nothing to reassure us that all our equipment is in perfect working order.

## On modesty

Seeing that I was one of the unlikely sirens, Ulysses rightly wasn't tempted. Instead, he sailed home.

## On timings

I'm sorry, Denis. Utterly unforgiveable. I assure you such a careless mistake will never happen again.

## On *Spartacus*

*Spartacus* went on for so long that our third child, a daughter, Andrea, who was born during the filming, was able to answer the questions of an inquisitive playmate before I had finished.
'What does your daddy do for a living?' asked the playmate.
'Spartacus,' replied Andrea.

## On real success

I will not hide the fact that the fun of having a play on is getting the box-office figures brought to me every night.

## On acting versus writing

To act well is, of course, difficult. But it is more difficult to write a bad play than to give a bad performance.

## On priests

Priests – and politicians for that matter – should regard themselves as entertainers at least in so far that it's the entertainer's primary task to keep the audience awake.

## On being a raconteur

It's about reducing a large theatre to the size of a drawing room. The trick is to look straight at an audience and make your eye wander so in the dark they all have the illusion you're picking them out. What you're really doing is thinking aloud, and immediately you start worrying, then you can't do it.

## On love scenes between real-life couples

Love scenes, and, even worse, lust scenes between people who presumably have them anyway in the privacy of their home are inevitably somewhat flat on the screen, and if they happen to be passing through a momentary crisis, such scenes are worse than flat, merely a tribute to their professionalism, and there are few things worse than that.

## On humour

If you can make people laugh, or at least amuse them, you have a chance of making contact. And I am defiantly an optimist, if only because the alternative is too dreadful to contemplate.

## On his writing plans

I hope to write more serious comedies and funnier tragedies than before.

## On raconteurs

The best raconteurs have the ability to be succinct and also, of course, to be tragi-comic, because you mustn't be frightened of moving people. That's a difference between a stand-up comic and raconteur. A raconteur should extract the pith out of life, in a sense, without being too pompous. He should really give you a sense of what life's all about.

## On comedians

One of the most ironic comedies of all is that great comedians are not comic in real life.

## On actors

Actors, on the whole, are often extremely shy people; there are, in fact, cases of actors who stammer and whose stammering disappears when they give a performance. The people who are really exhibitionists are lawyers, politicians, people who enjoy being themselves.

## On hecklers

The house-lights should immediately be trained on hecklers. Like owls they cannot hoot comfortably when illuminated.

### On hecklers

As witless cries reach you on the stage the first thing to remember is that you are being initiated into the magnificent company of men who have gone through it in the past and have survived with grace and humour.

### On hecklers

Novelists are better off than playwrights. You can't boo a bad book. Or if you do you run the risk of being regarded as eccentric.

## On comedy

Comedy is simply a funny way of being serious.

## On glamour

Glamour in the theatre usually means twenty chorus girls in a line all doing the same thing like a piece of machinery. It is assumed that twenty women are more glamorous than one.

## On making changes to his work

If there is one word wrong in a play of mine I flinch when I hear it. I can sense at once when something on the stage is not right. My nose twitches like a dog's.

### ON ACTING

As an actor, I stretch the possibilities of an audience to its limit.

### ON ACTING WITH YOUR OPPOSITE LEADING STAR

If you haven't complete rapport with the actress with whom you are acting it is like being thrust into the middle of a particularly edgy bullfight.

### ON PLEASING YOUR AUDIENCE

I believe that the theatre is a place where anything is permissible as long as the audience, in the main, is kept awake.

### On pleasing your audience

Putting on a play for the public is like opening the door to find a fierce dog behind it.

### On 'Acting and its effect on playwrights'

My interest in this subject is entirely passionate and therefore biased and therefore unreliable.

### On Shakespeare's clowns

It requires panache to be gay for a whole scene for no clear reason, with the additional strain of having to pretend to yourself that you know what you're talking about.

## On knowing one's lines

There is a deep-rooted conviction in the profession that a good text is one that is easy to learn. I don't believe it. I think that in common with most good things a good text is one that is difficult to learn, but even more difficult to forget.

## On praise

When I was twenty, we did not have the cult of the teenager and there was no particular merit in being twenty. At that age I had my first play produced and it was considered an impertinence rather than a phenomenon.

## ON PERFORMING IN KUALA LUMPUR

Since there seemed to be no theatres in Kuala Lumpur, I was compelled to do my one-man show in a hotel ballroom. My passport was returned to me later with the following entry:
'For performance as a comedian at the Concorde Hotel. Not permitted to sit out or dance with audience.'

## ON CRITICS

My second play, *Blow Your Own Trumpet,* was well and truly lacerated by the press – but not the public. They weren't there.

## On audience reactions

I shall always write as I think, even if I have to boo the gallery from the stage.

## On *Spartacus*

*Spartacus* must be the first film about an historical subject that took longer to make than the event it was about.

## On 'Sense of Humour'

Difficult to define in case you light on its mystery and destroy its innocence. But I would say that it's a readiness to see the funny side extant in everything.

## On 'Sense of the Ridiculous'

Thinking of the unfunny side of a situation first and then realizing its funny side immediately afterwards.

## On 'Sense of Comedy'

To contrast a situation with its unfunny side.

### On 'Sense of the Satirical'

To recognize all the above and then bring it home swiftly to a third party.

### On *The Egyptian*

Being in *The Egyptian* was like being an extra in an eternal performance of *Aida,* of which the music has been lost.

### On dismissing a film critic at Cannes Film Festival who was showing too much bias to director, Jean-Luc Godard

Waiting for Godard, no doubt?

## On having to learn foreign words in scripts

I'd rather be an actor than a linguistic stunt-man!

## On the advantage of film work

Theatre is the one dramatic art form left. TV is a corrupt and artificial substitute. I prefer film work to theatre because it usually allows a later start and offers something different every day.

## On movies

Movies are awfully like the army. There are in-trays, out-trays, the order of the day, and the hot brick of responsibility is thrown about with the speed of a football in a professional rugger match.

### ON TRADE UNIONS

I am a member of fourteen unions but I have never been on strike because all fourteen have never come out at the same time.

### ON FILM STUDIOS

Film studios are like nightclubs all over the world. Only the streets outside are different.

### ON LONDON THEATRE DURING WORLD WAR II

I was in Herbert Farjean's *Diversion,* for a while the only non-nude production playing in London.

## On playing Lear

Few things in life equal the sense of relief and achievement of those last minutes of *King Lear*, when the only obligation is to lie quite still, ignoring the fly ambling amongst the beads of perspiration on my nose.

## On theatre

What advantage does theatre enjoy over TV or films? Well, first of all it is the only form of entertainment which maintains a living contact with the audience. Consequently, in order to survive, it must create a kind of excitement, a kind of unpredictability . . .

### On being asked, while on tour with his one-man show, what he was reading

Road signs, mostly.

### On the secret of acting

The secret of acting is to reduce everything to absolute stillness because that gives the map scale. If you are absolutely still, when you move it registers; if you move the whole time, nothing registers.

### On critics

Critics search for ages for the wrong word which, to give them credit, they eventually find.

# *The Weakest Voices, The Best Ideas*

## ON ACTING IN THE DARK AFTER A POWER-CUT IN NEW ZEALAND

People's reactions in black obscurity were far more intense than they have ever been on any other occasion. There is a very good explanation. And, it is the reason why radio is still such a successful medium, since the listeners are forced to use their imagination, meeting the entertainer halfway.

### ON POVERTY

What sickens me most is the existence of poverty in wealthy countries and of wealthy people in poor countries. In each case it doesn't belong there.

### ON REVENGE

The trouble with the people who live for revenge is that they're never quite sure when they've had it – and so, to be on the safe side, they go on and on, endlessly.

### ON WISE MEN

No one can approach in imbecility the wise man besotted by his own wisdom.

## On style

Style is a way of lying. It is an ornament which hides the architecture.

## On knowing one's rights

To know one's rights is one thing. To exercise them is another.

## On expressing opinions

The more we are encouraged to express opinions, the fewer opinions we find there are to express. It is indicative that the largest turnout at elections are always where there is only one candidate.

## On choice

Where there is no choice all men are friends.

## On truth

Truth by its very nature is tendentious. Truth in Ghana is surely different from truth in the United States. To swear to tell the truth in a court of law would be impossible for me. I could only swear to tell *my* truth. The truth is really an ambition which is beyond us.

## On being a dramatist

The business of a dramatist is to ask questions – not to answer them.

## On Hectoring Producers and Directors

If a man shouts, his words no longer matter.

## On Sacred Causes

All nations have their altar-pieces of the mind. These are the deep-rooted causes of human conflict and gratuitous belligerency.

## On Capturing an Audience

I weighed nearly twelve pounds as a consequence of a reluctant and tardy birth. I have always been loath to acknowledge the applause of an audience unless its volume more than justifies such an initiative and I must have started the habit very early on, at my first public appearance in fact.

### On ideas

Those with the weakest voices often have the best ideas.

### On information

Information and disinformation travel at the same speed. In fact, our means of communication have improved so much that information doesn't 'travel' any more. It is there the same time as it happens.

### On humour

Laughter would be bereaved if snobbery died.

## On fairy stories

There is, of course, an endless delight in fairy stories. Especially as one grows older, the literary and human value of these flights of fancy begin to gain in profundity, and the frontiers between them and reality become more uncertain.

*Krumnagel*

## On conceit

In his brief interview with the Mayor, Krumnagel took care to explain his sensitivity about his age, without for a moment stooping to an apology.

The Mayor made light of the incident. 'None of us is perfect, Bart, as my old Greek mother used to say to me.'

Krumnagel thought the remark gratuitous, for though he did not have the sheer gall to consider himself perfect, he never for a moment entertained the idea that he might be in any way imperfect. It was strange the way this lousy Mayor had a gift for rubbing him up the wrong way.

*Krumnagel*

# Opera

On directing *The Rivals* in 1943 in Salisbury with Edith Evans as Mrs Malaprop ...

We had a happy mixture of civilian and military actors and, as an unexpected bonus, eight members of the Berlin Philharmonic orchestra, under their leader, Lance-Corporal Professor Doctor Reinhard Strietzel, and seven members of the Vienna Philharmonic, under their leader Private Professor Doctor Rudolf Stiasny, all now members of the Pioneer Corps, a section of the British army organized as a reserve of foreign talent, eager to do their bit against Hitler.

Rehearsals had their ups and downs. The orchestra seemed divided against itself, the first violin and conductor, Professor Strietzel, seeming to be at loggerheads with the first cello, Professor Stiasny, which culminated in an ugly scene, during which Lance-Corporal Strietzel threatened to put Professor Stiasny under close arrest. He pointed to the single stripe on his arm with the tip of his bow, calling out in a thick German accent, 'You know vat zis means?' The conflict was complicated by the intervention of Edith Evans. As they filed out of their rehearsal hall to make way for the mummers, Professor Strietzel looked at poor Edith and said, 'I don't know . . . how all zis . . . shall end!'

One drawback of those garrison theatres was that there was no method of concealing the orchestra. Its members sat on the same level as the audience. It was merely the actors who were elevated. I noticed on the first night that the orchestra made use of a miniature chessboard in order to while away the time during the histrionics, and often musicians crept forward like troops in a dugout to make a move. As far as I could understand it, it was a permanent championship: Berlin versus Vienna.

I hoped and prayed that Edith Evans wouldn't notice what was going on, but on the fourth night, during a brilliant tirade, she stopped dead. One eye had alighted on the tiny chessboard just as an Austrian viola player had spotted a crack in the enemy defence, and was creeping forward to deliver the coup de grâce. She was livid, and after the show I accosted Professor Strietzel.

To soften the blow somewhat I told him he had never played better than on that night.

His face lit up. 'You are a real musician,' he counter-flattered.

'There's only one thing . . . one criticism.'

'Ach!' His face darkened.

'The game of chess. It's frightfully distracting?'

'It distracts you?'

'Yes.'

'No!' he roared. 'You are too fine an artist to be distracted. It's zis voman!'

The next night Edith found it hard to concentrate, which was quite unlike her. As soon as I came on stage I saw what was happening. The orchestra, deprived of its chessboard, had now arranged the lights on its music-stands so that its members were lit from beneath, and they all followed Edith's every move in this ghostly light, looking like war criminals following the arguments of their advocate with misgiving and resignation.

Once again, at the end of the performance, I was compelled to accost Professor Strietzel. 'I have a criticism.'

'Please?'

'Why do you follow Edith Evans with your eyes in a manner calculated to disturb any performer, any artist?'

'First it vas the chessboard. Correct me if I am wrong. Chess ve shouldn't play . . .'

'That is correct.'

'So ve leave the chessboard at home. Vot else can ve do? Ve follow the play. Ve look at the voman.'

Suddenly the constriction of his voice and the coolness of presentation of the facts deserted him. He shouted volcanically, 'You think it gives us pleasure to vatch zis voman? Ve who have seen Paula Wessely at her height?'

The next night Edith was brilliant. The only trouble was the entire absence of laughs. I made my entrance, and, inspired by the zest and brio of Edith, I acted as well as I knew how, in complete and utter silence. It was acutely depressing. Not even the presence of three generals in the front row could justify the extraordinary dullness of the audience. When I had a free moment, I rushed to the back of the auditorium to unravel the mystery. I did not have far to seek. The musicians had now reversed their positions, and sat facing the audience, their heads just visible above the rail of the orchestra pit. Lit from beneath, like mournful skittles waiting for the usual knocks of fate, they had utterly dampened the spirits of the onlookers.

# *Eureka!*

## ON HAPPINESS

I am at my happiest with imperfect happiness. Perfection has no personality.

## ON SATISFYING YOUR CURIOSITY

An artist can always exercise his curiosity on the grounds of a search for material.

### On patience

Take your time. To be in a hurry is to kill your talent. If you wish to reach the sun it isn't enough to jump impulsively into the air.

### On the perfect story

The most brilliant I ever heard was from a taxi driver in Toronto who was driving me through the snow to the airport. He suddenly said to me, 'I lost my wife', and I prepared to be sympathetic, ' . . . to my best friend, Jim. I don't care about her but I sure miss him. Well, thank God I still got Mother'. That is perfect to me because you understand the point of view of the wife, the lover, him and the mother. It puts them all into context in the most economical way possible.

## On staying calm

A state of calm preserves your energy and enables you to go on being calm without undue effort.

## On how to relax

I relax by going to bed and contemplating the ceiling. I would contemplate my navel like an Oriental mystic, only I can't see that far.

## On weight

I have always been a heavy-weight. When I was born, I tipped the scales at 12lb.

95 THESES
BY
MARTIN
LUTHER

CONFOUND IT. I'VE JUST THOUGHT
OF A 96TH THESIS

## On democracy

The Greeks didn't invent democracy, they did something much more valuable; they lived it and then eventually they found a word to describe it. Democracy is something to be guarded very jealously.

## On politicians and the weather

Politicians resemble weathermen who . . . predict . . . bright intervals during a day of unrelieved rain.

## On time

It is a cliché that the elderly judge contemporary life by the yardstick of a real or imagined past. Memory, they say, plays tricks, and the events of a bygone age acquire a mellow patina like antique furniture. Even the most terrible events are recollected by those who survived them with a tenderness which suggests that time itself creates reverence as it passes.

## On *Mona Lisa*

I think the *Mona Lisa* is highly overrated. She looks like the matron in an inferior hospital, with a sort of mind-over-matter look. Perhaps da Vinci painted her as a target for his siege-machinery?

## On beginner's luck

I'm a great believer in beginner's luck. That's why I try so many things.

## On happiness

I am probably very happy because I am never content.

## On reaching the wrong conclusion

I know one or two actors who are homely enough for it to be assumed that because they look so plain they must be good actors – and they're not.

## On mimicry

People discern a basic goodwill in what I do and don't take offence.

## On art

When I was in the army, I was asked to write the programme notes for an art exhibition for the princely sum of five pounds. It went to my head completely and I lay on the floor in some commandeered boarding house on the south coast and wrote my article by the light of a flickering pocket torch. I went back to the gallery and found an atmosphere of great gloom – they had gone bankrupt and could not pay me. Seeing my distress and the fact that I was in uniform – which was a certain advantage in that period of history - they gave me something out of stock which I took away in disgust and didn't look at it for about thirty years when I discovered it to be a large watercolour by Oskar Kokoschka and very valuable.

## On the Arts

The arts are one of the few known antidotes to the pallor of accuracy and the frigid exhilaration of scientific techniques.

## On Being Creative in Cars

Cars are the modern equivalent of the bath although it is much more dangerous to jump out of a moving car shouting, 'Eureka!'

# *But a Ball Makes My Teeth Grate*

## On Playing Tennis with a Belly

I don't consider my stomach a handicap in tennis. It's a kind of secret weapon. People don't expect people with a paunch like mine to be agile on the courts. It takes them by surprise when I dash, and don't waddle, to the net. I'm used to dealing with my problem on court. If I became thin I would be completely off-balance, and bang would go my secret weapon!

### On patriotism

Practically every game played internationally today was invented in Britain, and when foreigners became good enough to match or even defeat the British, the British quickly invented a new game.

### On the British

The Englishman likes to feel that he can laugh at himself. He only does this, however, to take all the pleasure out of laughing at him.

### On walking at airports

Airports I hate. You have to walk miles. I see people passing in wheelchairs and then my jealousy turns to hatred when they get to the aeroplane and they jump up and walk down the aisle.

### THE ENGLISH

The English sportsman prides himself on being a good loser; by being this, he makes sure his opponents feel guilty for having won.

### ON WAR

In war you know damn well that it is your sacred duty to kill the other fellow before you have time to find out if you have a common interest or not.

### ON CRICKET

An irritating game which I loathed mainly on account of the ball being much too hard.

## On cricket

I know that cricket has inspired many great Englishmen: I can't help it that the sound of bat on ball makes my teeth grate.

## On beards

In filming, a beard is a practical thing. You save one hour every morning in make-up and can therefore sleep longer. Counting on an average film, that amounts to about one hundred extra hours of sleep. It is the actor's only bonus over the audience. No film allows an audience to sleep as long as that.

## On being asked how much he earned in civvy street

I told him that since I was self-employed, my earning would fluctuate. He patiently renewed his question, as though dealing with some dim-witted colonial.

'It's not too difficult to understand,' he crooned in his lilting Scots accent. 'I merely wished to know your weekly income in time of peace.'

I told him I understood his question, and would make every effort to make the answer as simple.

'Since I am an actor and a writer, I have no regular employment. I very often make nothing in a week –' I attempted a laugh, in which he failed to join. 'When I do make something, it is of a variable or inconsistent nature.'

He closed his eyes as though summoning hidden reserves of patience, and breathed deeply.

'I don't know why you are making this so difficult,' he murmured in a clenched voice. 'I merely asked you the extent of your pay cheque at the end of every week.'

'And that is precisely the question to which I cannot give you an accurate answer,' I replied between my gritted teeth. 'You must have heard of an actor having a bad year. Well, a bad year is made up of a preponderance of bad weeks over good weeks. By the same token, a good year is made up of a preponderance of good weeks over

bad weeks. It surely stands to reason that it is impossible to give mean ratio of good and bad weeks because I haven't been going that long.'
He sighed, and looked up at the ceiling as though something of rare interest were going on up there. I declined to follow his gaze, since I knew perfectly well that nothing at all was going on up there.'Let me phrase my question differently,' he said at length.

## ON ARMY UNIFORMS

In my army uniform I looked like the loser in a sack-race.

### On watching 'Rome' burn on the set of *Quo Vadis*

Green rivers rolled down my face formed by the inferior metal they used to make my laurel wreath melting in the heat of the flames and it being the hottest day of the year. The American actress who was supposed to pluck at her harp as I played on my lyre said, 'Honey, you just do anything you want with your hands and I'll follow yer.'

### On tennis

I see the ball coming and I think to myself, 'I have plenty of time to reach that', and it bounces three times before I have fallen down.

## On laziness

I look back astounded at memories of the film *Quo Vadis,* and realize that oysters are not the only creatures drawn towards either an inherent or acquired taste for immobility. On the hottest day of this century, the lions were supposed to devour the Christians in the Colosseum. I remember every detail of this since, as Nero, I had the best seat in the arena. I gave the thumbs down signal for the games to begin. There was a roar from the crowd as the lions ambled into the violent sunshine of the stadium. A few seconds later they formed a queue to return to the sepulchral shade of their cages, and even the fact that they had not eaten for a couple of days did nothing to help them direct a few somnolent paces towards the crucified Christians, who were in fact dolls packed with raw meat.

## ON 'LEARNING LINES'

In my early days in the Army I was always picked as a runner on exercises and had to charge all over huge fields delivering vital messages. They made me a runner because they assumed that, as an actor, I could remember long messages. But I was always so exhausted that I hadn't the breath to deliver the message. When I'd recovered my breath I'd forgotten it.

## ON FOOTBALL

Is it not absurd, and woefully anti-climactic, to allow a splendid match to terminate in the arbitrary lottery of shoot-outs? It is as though a great war (of the obsolete, invigorating type) were to end, not with a meeting of minds over the conference table but in a game of Russian roulette played by selected private soldiers of both sides.

## ON TENNIS COMMENTATORS AROUND THE WORLD

Their description of what we can see with our own eyes is charged with private jokes, hit-or-miss sparkle and a habit of getting Czechs, Yugoslavs and Russians hopelessly muddled, to say nothing of Peruvians, Argentinians and Chileans. Switch to a German channel and there are rather fewer inside jokes. No jokes at all, in fact. . . The British, on the whole, give the viewers credit for having eyes in their heads, and, therefore, talk rather less than their colleagues from other lands. Also, the British have the enormous advantage of having no one to root for after the first round.

BEFORE THE START OF THE 1ST 4 x 100 METRES RELAY RACE AT THE OLYMPIC GAMES

## ON EXERCISE

Exercise, the voluntary exhaustion of the human mechanism, is partly due to the speed of life, the need for lightning reactions in many fields of existence. The new obsession with diets and physical well-being, expressed in many ways from *cuisine minceur* to jogging and that orgy of hopping and skipping enjoying the typical pseudo-scientific name of aerobics, is a valid reflection of the preoccupations of today.

# *A Form of Incontinence*

## On writing

I act for a living. I write because I must.

## On deadlines

The ideal playwright would, like a dog who buries a bone, leave it for a time and, when he has a free moment, from time to time, dig it up. I, too, need to be miserly with my ideas to store and rake them over.

### On tedium

After eight hundred performances of *Love and Four Colonels* I had become a zombie. I'd say words like 'Together' and wonder whether I had pronounced it properly.

### On writing

I don't believe you can be an angry writer. Anger gets in the way of the plot, and you are no longer creating real characters. You must never forget that you have to be the Devil's Advocate as well.

### On writing

It is a form of incontinence.

### On writing

Writing is tough; what is difficult is to know when to stop.

## ON LANGUAGE

English is fine for not saying what you actually mean. French is precise, whereas English is the language of get-out clauses.

## ON PLAYS

The first copy of a finished play is rather like a pair of new shoes. They – and it – will look scruffy in ten minutes.

## ON WRITING

Too many authors are like fish or birds that want to swim or fly in one direction, change course at the same time and behave alike at the same seasons.

### ON WRITING

All writers have a maternal instinct. They cherish the weakest of their creations.

### ON WRITING

I consider myself a writer first and foremost. Acting is intrinsically easier than writing. To act well is, of course, difficult but I think it is more difficult to write a bad play than give a bad performance, to put it at its lowest level.

### ON GETTING STARTED IN A TELEVISION INTERVIEW

When you are taking part in a television interview show the commercials always come on just as you are settling down and beginning to sound like Voltaire. I guarantee Voltaire wouldn't have stood for it.

## On typing

If I could type I would rather play the harpsichord. My mind works at the speed of a pen.

## On the media

The great blight of the contemporary political leader is over-exposure, which any actor knows is a misfortune almost as difficult to bear as under-exposure. Over-exposure leads to the kind of familiarity which breeds contempt for those of discernible personality and indifference to all others. Prime ministers of the past could have said more or less what they pleased in a London club, and it would probably have gone no further. Now the club itself invites the media to share their privilege, and for the media, read the public.

# *Hearing Voices*

## ON GOD

It is becoming increasingly obvious that God is no longer with us. Up till now man has been tormented with questions to which there have been no answers; because of computers we are being showered with answers to which we have not even put the questions.

## ON CAPITAL PUNISHMENT

The death sentence is a misnomer. There is no death sentence; it is merely a sentence to spend the last days of life as unpleasantly as possible.

### ON THATCHER

The difference between Maggie Thatcher and Joan of Arc is that Thatcher only hears her own voice.

### ON LINGUISTS

People who know too many languages rarely have much to say in any of them.

### ON GROWING OLDER

As I grow older I find that though I think I'm saying the same things as I always did, people listen to me more.

MRS. THATCHER HEARING
HER VOICE

## On acts of God

In order to complain about a tidal wave you have to be on more intimate terms with the Almighty than any mere mortal can be.

## On religion

Religion is blackmail. It holds a man's opinion of himself to ransom.

## On the best environment for writing

I must have music when I'm writing. It is probably because I started my writing career during the war and thus had to concentrate to a background of noise from bombing. Now I find silence unbearable and must have radio or even television on all the time. Occasionally I look up and see Bette Davis taking poison but it doesn't distract me.

## On the best environment for writing

To someone who is concentrating hard on writing a play there is really no difference between the telephone and a bomb, except that the bomb you can't answer. So that, really, unless it's a direct hit, I prefer bombs to the telephone as music to write by.

## On dogs

A dog will always be a better friend to man than other men. But even here the thoroughbred is often more highly prized than the mongrel, which is as tactful an outlet for racialism as any.

## On temptation

Temptation given in to promptly is no longer temptation. Temptation only comes with the second thought.

## On vice

I have found no vice that appeases me for longer than it takes to perform it.

## On being Christian

It is hard for a Christian to survive in a Godless society. The first casualty in a Godless society is always the Devil and without the Devil a Christian is lost.

## On doubt

Doubts are the spurs of thoughts. The more I know what I am supposed to think the less I know what I really think.

## On American politics

In America, through pressure of conformity, there is freedom of choice, but nothing to choose from.

## On United States diplomacy

At times the United States are about as elegant as an elephant dancing on its points.

## On the origin of democracy

Americans believe that freedom was their invention. They have been known to send peace-corps groups to Athens to teach the Greeks the meaning of the word democracy.

### On democracy

American democracy is like that of a rich man who hails the porter at his apartment block. 'Hi, Tom!' (his name's really Jack) 'How are the kids, Tom?' (he has no children) Yet both parties are pleased with this friendly transaction.

### On American politics

I once wrote a short story which wasn't published because of the accusation of hitting President Johnson below the belt. It's hardly my fault if LBJ wears his belt like a crown.

### On being a translator

When a man has too many faculties, he ends up qualifying as a translator with the United Nations.

### On liberals

In America a Liberal is a kind of embryonic 'Commie', a nuisance who asks subversive and embarrassing questions.

### On liberals

The main weakness of the Liberals in Britain is that their platform is occupied by both other parties.

### On foreign affairs

In the Foreign Office I visualize a small room where people are taught to stutter.

## On voting

Not to vote is not necessarily a sign of laziness or lack of civic sense. It may be an expression of opinion. And, as such, deserves the respect accorded a vote for a candidate.

## On democracy

The difference between an ordinary democracy and a people democracy is that in a people's democracy opinion cannot be freely expressed and therefore goes unheeded, whereas in an ordinary democracy like those in the West, opinion can be freely expressed and therefore goes unheeded.

## On American politics

In the case of the American Presidency it is the machine which drives the driver and the driver is only required to make reassuring gestures of being in charge of the machine.

## ON THE DANGER OF INSTANT REACTIONS

In the past the errors of princes, blunders of kings and indiscretions of politicians had the time and space in which to fade before reaching their destination. It was still possible to reconsider words and phrases to appeal to reason. But now we live in an age of instant reactions . . .

# *Love Thy Neighbour, but Build a Wall*

## ON PREJUDICE

Is there not a unity in the composition of humanity? If a baby is crying next door, we cannot tell its colour or its race by the sound of its voice, its only means of expression. The raw material is the same until the the prejudices of tradition begin to erode virgin sensibilities, and a particular view of history identifies longstanding enmities.

## On common ground

Most of us are generally united by our doubts and divided by our convictions.

## On old men behaving badly

Whenever old men behave badly, it is invariably their youthful souls which fail to realize, either mistakenly or deliberately, the extent of their physical decrepitude. It is this depressing fact which creates so-called 'dirty old men' whose watering pupils dilate with every passing cleavage or quivering buttock.

## On being asked to be linesman at Wimbledon Tennis Championship

I excused myself by expressing myself flattered by the offer, but begged them to renew it when my eyesight had deteriorated sufficiently for me to be able to make wrong decisions with absolute conviction.

## On linesmen in general

Eventually, linesmen, faced by the the extraordinary speed of the modern game, will be eliminated altogether and replaced by computers, which have the virtue of being capable of errors far grosser than human ones, but which are not open to appeal.

### On defining NATO

Six nations in search of an enemy.

### On defining NATO

Like a dinosaur. A tiny brain and an enormous body.

### On not killing

When I was a child in Estonia my family used to make its own yoghurt. My uncle had a sensible passion for keeping the flies off it. But when I took to fly-swatting with a vengeance, he reproved me saying, 'It is better that we should be slightly ill than you should acquire a taste for killing.'

THE MILITARY OPTION, THEN AND NOW

WAR NEVER LOOKS GOOD ON RETROSPECT

### On war

War never looks good in retrospect, when the errors of judgment and prevalent doubts begin to be uncovered by historians. And the prosecution of war is even more costly than its prevention. The Cold War! Those were restful days. At least you knew where you stood.

### On old enmities

A Russian and a Polish labourer repairing a derelict house chance upon a horde of gold. The Russian says eagerly, 'We'll share it like brothers.' 'No,' replies the Pole, 'fifty-fifty.'

### On the making of a good speech

The key to a good speech is to have a brilliant beginning, a brilliant ending and keep them as close as possible.

## On traditional wisdom

Three Russian proverbs
'Love thy neighbour but build a wall.' 'The road to the church is icy; so is the road to the tavern, but I will walk carefully.' 'When engaged in a fight, it is not the moment to part your hair.'

## On philosophers

Philosophers are more interested in money than are financiers, for the very valid reason that they have less of it.

## On history (from *Add a Dash of Pity*)

You are looking at the world through the eyes of a historian . . . but the world is not run by historians. It is a luxury we cannot afford. We can't study events from such a comfortable distance nor can we allow ourselves to be embittered by the unfortunate parallels and repetitions of history.

## ON THE LEGAL PROFESSION (FROM *ADD A DASH OF PITY*)

Damn the legal profession. . . What do they do? For the purposes of argument they take a completely extraordinary event, full of extraordinary and perverted aspects, and make it sound ordinary and natural.

## ON DIPLOMACY

A diplomat these days is nothing but a headwaiter who's allowed to sit down occasionally.

*Romanoff and Juliet*

# *It's Dangerous to Lean out of Windows*

## ON FOOLING THE SYSTEM

My father was an extraordinary man when it came to money. He somehow managed to live all his life with the gusto and philanthropy of an extremely wealthy man – without being burdened with the many complications of actually possessing any money.

## ON OPTIMISM AND PESSIMISM

An optimist is one who knows exactly how sad the world can be, while a pessimist is one who finds out anew every morning.

## ON MONEY

Money corrupts – particularly those who don't have any.

## ON ADVICE TO TREASURE

*E pericoloso sporgersi* (it is dangerous to lean out of the window).

## On money

I think of money only when I have none left. My greatest luxury is to forget that it exists.

## On his flight from Manchester–London

In the words of a stewardess on the London–Manchester flight
'In the unlikely eventuality of a landing on water – ' It would take a damned good pilot to pull that one off; or one with absolutely no sense of direction.

## ON THE CHANGING FACE OF VILLAINS

In Italy they have actually begun to seize documents at the most illustrious masonic lodges in search of links with organized crime. America has had a glut of sharepushers and the kind of Robin Hoods who rob the rich in order to keep the money themselves. Britain has had Maxwell and the Guinness saga, while France struggles with the miserable tale of doctors responsible for diffusion of blood contaminated by the AIDS virus. Prisons are filling up with smart people.

## ON HOW YOU TICK

I never stand aside and look at myself in case I find out how I tick.

## ON *QUO VADIS*

A miniature of Rome caught fire to add to the inferno, and a back-projection screen came alive with visual pyrotechnics behind us. At last we were ready to shoot. I recalled the words of my crazed song, 'O Lambent flames, O force divine', and cleared what throat I could still sense. Just then Mervyn [Leroy, the director] cried, 'Let me down! Let me down, for Christ's sake, will you?'

A sense of exasperated anti-climax set in as Mervyn disappeared from sight. Then the balcony began to shake, indicating someone was scaling it. Mervyn's head appeared over the battlements, cigar gripped between his teeth, his eyes confident and understanding like those of a manager telling a half-dead boxer that he's leading on points, and he summoned me to within confidential distance.

Waving his Havana at the burning city in *Quo Vadis,* he said quietly. 'Don't forget, you're responsible for all this.' Mervyn was never a director to leave anything to chance.

## ON MODESTY

Modesty is the unhealthiest form of introspection.

## ON THE TALENT HE WOULD LIKE TO HAVE

The ability to decipher double talk.

## ON THE MOST OVERRATED VIRTUE

Qualities of leadership. The German word for leader is Führer.

## ON MONEY

I never worry about revealing my earnings to the taxman. Why should he worry? After all, he gets it all.

## ON HIPPIES

The reason they are like this is because they are trying to find the essential goodness we lost on the way to civilization.

## ON EVIL

Things only become evil when they are no longer funny.

## On bombs

Have you noticed that bombs are called 'devices' when they don't explode?

## On pornography

Pornography is a release rather than an encouragement. It is lack of imagination that makes people revel in pornography.

## On LSD

It provides the same hallucination that a medieval nun once obtained by starving.

### On loyalty

I can pledge no allegiance to a flag until I know who is holding it.

### On ambition

My ambitions are impressive, but also mainly secret. However, I admit to one ambition. I would like to make enough money to enable me to afford to live the way I do live.

### On folly

In this age of mass-communication, folly is contagious.

## On mortality (from *The Old Man and Mr Smith*)

Mortality gives the world its yardstick of quality. If Beethoven had been immortal there would have been thousands of symphonies infinitely repetitive and eventually indistinguishable from each other even in degrees of mediocrity.

## On prejudice

Prejudice is an indefinable weed which is at its most insidious in the greenest of lawns.

## On behaviour

This is a free country, madam. We have a right to share your privacy in a public place.

*Romanoff and Juliet*

## On entertaining

He believed utterly in democracy in which even the poorest and darkest had the vote, but in which only the richest and whitest could be voted for. He believed in it because he had neither the capacity nor the inclination to entertain any other beliefs. All he was able to entertain were guests, which he did without respite, and apparently without fatigue.

*Krumnagel*

# School Reports

## ON BEING LAZY

I am fundamentally lazy. I am very, very lazy. I was accused of being lazy at school. And my father accused me of being lazy. Everybody accused me of being lazy - and a procrastinator, and I work quite hard in order to prove to myself - unsuccessfully - that I am not lazy.

## On education

Education is important, especially in alleviating prejudice. If you are going to be a prisoner of your own mind, the least you can do is to make sure that your cell is well-furnished.

## On saluting

London was a nightmare for private soldiers, since there seemed to be someone to salute every ten yards.

## On school reports

I have never quite recovered from the psychological impact of a school report I received which I would not have believed possible had my mother not shown it to me. It read: 'This boy shows great originality, which must be curbed at all cost.'

## ON LEARNING

It is of primordial importance to learn more every year than the year before.

## ON THE BEST EDUCATION

Any child worth his salt will learn more by reaction against than obedience to.

## ON EDUCATION

Education is not confined to school. It continues relentlessly to the end of life.

### On nationality

Because I had a German passport, at school I was always regarded with some suspicion as the boy who lost the last war.

### On Ustinov, according to Rebecca West

She said I was good, but not up to my father.

### On punishments

I was quite a nice child, I think, except that when other children misbehaved I gather they were threatened with me as a playmate.

### ON PROFESSIONS

I've often thought people reach the top of the tree because they haven't got the qualifications to detain them at the bottom. A very good lawyer tends to stay in the law. The one who's not quite as gifted becomes Richard Nixon.

### ON INSPIRING HIS SECRETARY

I must have inspired her with my own brilliant disorder, for she got her own back by writing a play which was very, very good.

### ON MAKING UP THE NUMBERS

When I was a child I used to play a flute, not because I loved it, but because there was a shortage of flautists in the school orchestra.

## On big lips

I've got rather a large upper lip; consequently when I played the flute I very often got the right notes but invariably got the wrong octave. Somehow, in Handel's *Messiah*, this fault stood out.

## On British education

British education is probably the best in the world if you can survive it; if you can't, there's nothing left for you but the diplomatic corps.

NOSTALGIA FOR
SHEPHERD'S PIE

## On nostalgia

I certainly miss some things from school, enormously at times. Like that odious custard, and that shepherd's pie, so horrid. Yet I occasionally have great nostalgia to taste it again, rather, I suppose, as a criminal returns to the scene of his crime.

## On school

School is only the place where you learn to learn. So it becomes a useful pastime at a period of life when the mind needs such a pastime.

# Changing the Subject

## On Announcing Your Engagement

There's nothing more suitable to announce your engagement to your friends than a nice religious postcard. It takes away all frivolous aspects of the negotiation, and has a spontaneous dignity which no amount of subsequent teasing can ever dispel.

### On family rivalry

My father started hundreds of novels but never, ever, got past the first page. I don't think he ever quite forgave me when my first play was produced, not because I had got it on, but because I had actually *finished* something.

### On irony

There are two countries in the world where irony doesn't exist: America and Monaco. The first because it is too big, the second because it is too small.

## On Avoiding Publicity

How lucky were the great men of the past! They could disappear for a while to let dust settle, to let things blow over when they had gone wrong. Today there is no respite. The camera lies in wait in the most unexpected places. We know all our candidates far too well for their own comfort, their own peace of mind. Popularities fluctuate as hysterically as values on the Stock Exchange as we notice some detail which displeases us, or a casual *faux-pas* is blown into a national calamity by the media.

## On Democracy

Corruption is nature's way of restoring our faith in democracy.

### ON CAREERS

My father wanted me to be a lawyer but I told him I was going into the theatre, which is the same job, really – but less dangerous to my fellow men.

### ON CORRUPTION

I suppose that tipping a head waiter before a meal is corrupt since the diner expects special treatment in return for his investment, whereas the same sum slipped into the head waiter's discreetly cupped hand after a meal is merely gratitude, for services rendered and therefore not corrupt.

Peter Ustinov as Hercule Poirot in Agatha Christie's *Evil Under the Sun.* EMI 1982 (Courtesy Kobal)

Ustinov opposite Elizabeth Taylor in *Beau Brummel.* M-G-M 1954 (Courtesy Kobal)

Ustinov with (*left to right*) Aldo Ray, Humphrey Bogart, and Leo G. Carroll in *We're No Angels.* Paramount 1954 (Courtesy Kobal)

Ustinov shares a scene with Melvyn Douglas in *Billy Budd.* Allied Artists 1962 (Courtesy Kobal)

In a scene from *Logan's Run* Peter Ustinov joins co-stars Michael York and Jenny Agutter. M-G-M 1975 (Courtesy Kobal)

Ustinov is flanked by David Niven and Bette Davis in a scene from *Death on the Nile*. EMI 1978 (Courtesy Kobal)

In *The Sundowners* Ustinov shares a scene with Deborah Kerr. Warner Brothers 1960 (Courtesy Kobal)

Peter Ustinov in *Romanoff and Juliet.* Universal 1961 (Courtesy Kobal)

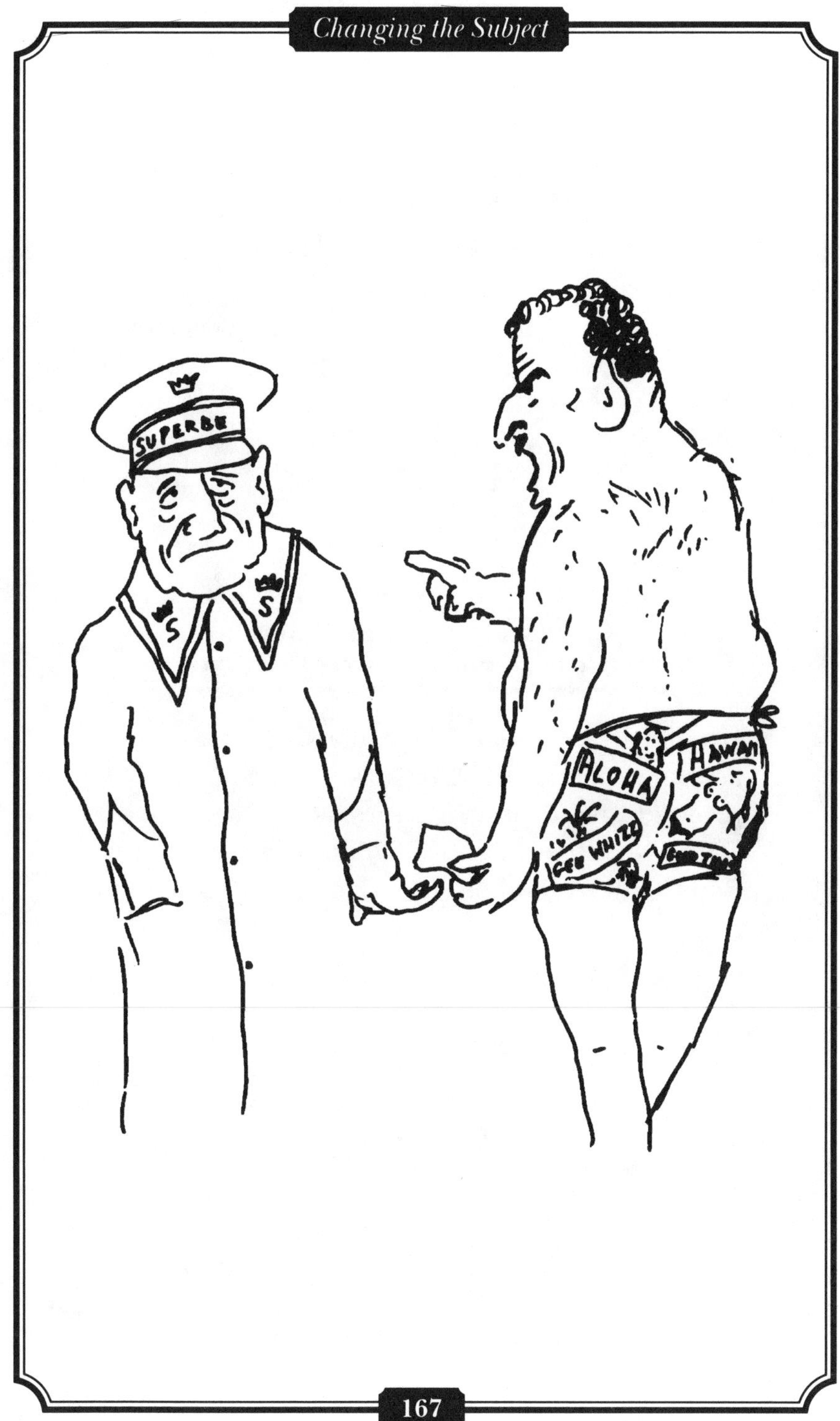
SUPERBE
S
S
ALOHA

### On being in the army

Four and a half years in the British Army was the longest role I've every played; grossly underpaid and I was miscast, but it was a big spectacular and a very long run.

### On his boat *Christina*, before changing her name to *Nitchevo*

[It] led to endless complications, since that was also the name of Onassis's floating place. I received a few cryptic messages by mistake, such as: 'Time Not Ripe Baghdad Willing Suggest Twenty Repeat Twenty Million Adequate Karakristidis.'

## On being Rector of Dundee University

Of all the memories I took away from there which gave me a personal glow of satisfaction, the most disarming came from a distressed parent appealing for consideration for his wayward child. The envelope was addressed to 'The Lord Rectum of Dundee University', and that is how I have seen myself ever since in moments of self-doubt.

## On being chosen a Rector of Dundee University

I had never been to Dundee before. That's probably why they chose me to be rector of their university.

## On daughters

I have three daughters and I find as a result I played King Lear almost without rehearsal.

## On bringing up children

I never encouraged my children to be creative. A parent's example is much more eloquent than anything you can say to them. I have never tried to help them by influence. Even their disappointments should be their own but I will help materially.

## On paternal feeling

I was a constant source of disappointment to my father. When I managed to pass an audition at the Players' club, giving a turn as the Bishop of Limpopo, my father said: 'Not even drama – *vaudeville*!'

## ON *QUO VADIS*

I was playing my lyre while an Italian girl was cutting my toenails - the actress was subsequently named as co-respondent in the Barbara Stanwyck /Robert Taylor divorce, which I found extraordinary as she wasn't much to look at. However, she was supposed to nick my toe just as I reached a searingly high note on the lyre, at which I had to kick her across the marble floor so she started to bleed. I then had to say, 'Take her away before she leaks to death.' I ventured to say to the director it was an unpleasant line and he had to cable head office and alter the shooting schedule before a decision could be made.

## ON BEING SHOCKING

I believe it is a form of decadence merely to be shocking. Shock works on the nerves and not on the intellect and any idea which has to rely on pulling at the nervous system is decadent.

### On the benefits of being the producer, Walt Disney

If one of his characters became difficult all he had to do was to erase it.

### On changing times

The Renaissance followed the Dark Ages simply because there was no other way for civilization to survive. Today we are faced with a situation quite as dramatic, and where the discovery of a new direction for the human race is as urgent as ever it has been.

### On America's preoccupation with health

In American most people now have an annual check-up every month.

### On America's preoccupation with health

Medicine is largely preventative in the States. If you need a cure it only shows you haven't taken enough vitamin shots, which proves that you're careless and stupid.

### On history

You, sir, talked of Columbus. In his day, men for all their culture, fine paintings, architecture, humanism, the rest, were still relatively savage. Life was cheap. Death was the penalty for a slight misdemeanour, slavery the penalty for an accident of birth. Why? Because there was space to conquer, horizons full of promise.

*The Man in the Moon*

## ON STANDARDS

There are never as few as double standards at work. Standards are as variable as the weather, and deserve a scale of their own, taking in to consideration local conditions, prevailing prejudice, climatic changes and precedents.

*The Disinformer*

## ON HOSTAGES

Hostages had been taken long before Richard Coeur de Lion languished in an Anatolian castle waiting for ransom to be paid. Innocents have been massacred from the dawn of recorded history, and still today men, women and children are killed, not as a result of their culpability, but as an example to others. To be permanently shocked by such events is to be ignorant of history, or else it is just demagogic humbug.

*The Disinformer*

## On Pavarotti

Pavarotti is not vain, but conscious of being unique.

## On generals

As for being a general, well at the age of four with paper hats and wooden swords we're all generals. Only some of us never grow out of it.

HOLLYWOOD
MEN

# Hollywood

## On Hollywood

In Los Angeles one gets a certain nostalgia for England. There are certain mornings when vision is restricted by a deep lifeless smog. Then one can forget all the travel posters and almost cheerfully believe that one is back in Uxbridge or even Slough.

## On Hollywood

Few Hollywood top executives seem sure of their friends, but they all seem absolutely sure of their enemies.

## On Hollywood men

Hollywood is full of men of fifty who look after themselves with such assiduous application that they look like a very healthy sixty.

## On Hollywood parties

A host in Hollywood is someone who is never quite sure who will turn up.

## On Hollywood parties

I considered that I had beaten the system when one head waiter whispered to me:
'Where's your coat, Mr Ustinov? I'll put it somewhere handy. I doubt if you'll want to stay here very long.'

## On Hollywood

Hollywood represents the true democracy of art, in which the ignoramus with the gift of instinct argues it out with the professor crammed with knowledge and rancid ideals.

## On Hollywood

Walking in Hollywood is tantamount to loitering with intent.

# *A Midwife Needs a Baby*

## ON COMPUTER TECHNOLOGY

A Danish lady of one hundred and four was summoned to enrol in a nursery school the other day, because the computer only went up to ninety-nine, and she appeared on the records as being five years old.

### ON GIRLS' FASHIONS

The dirtiest periods in history were when most was covered – like the Victorian era. Today, it's all strip and no tease, and that cannot be altogether a bad thing. Then, it was thirty minutes' strip and the perils of the cupboard if the husband returned unexpectedly.

### ON GRAFFITI

Modern graffiti are either illegible, incomprehensible or vulgar. If they happen to have been sprayed on a hard surface they seem to have been executed by the same neurotic hand, that of a disturbed pastrycook perhaps, who bestrides the world with his urgent messages.

## On modern alarm clocks

Your modern alarm clock produces a lady's voice which tells you in dehumanized terms that it is 6.15. You thought you were sharing your bed with your wife until this jarring foretaste of a ménage à trois enters your orbit with a human warmth reminiscent of matron at school.

## On computers

Some people say computers are better than people – but they don't get much fun out of life.

## On change

Change comes with the erosion of established ideas, like the tireless gnawing at cliffs by the sea. Our concept of the future is often felicitous, because we cannot foresee the emergence of new texture, of new techniques and, consequently, of new appearances.

## On occupational necessities

A midwife needs a baby and an undertaker needs a corpse; and an insurance company needs an occasional embezzler to remind them what they're in business for.

## On couples

No man should be alone to face huge horizons. Even in Noah's Ark there were no bachelors or spinsters among the animals.

## On his boat, *Nitchevo*

It can sleep six people who know each other very well. Or one prude.

## ON BEING FAT

'Fat' has been a dirty word and fallen into disrepute. It used to mean 'abounding in riches, well-furnished, well-filled out'. Now it just means 'not slim'.

## ON CONDUCTING

Someone gave me a baton when I was young. Since then I've conducted practically every big orchestral work – in front of a radiogram.

## ON TALENT

It is not enough for a country to breed talent. It must eventually deserve it.

### On equality of the sexes

Complete equality between the sexes doesn't work unless tempers are equable – and who ever heard of a woman as even-tempered as a man?

### On bachelors

Our Lord was a bachelor, and it's safe to assume that his instructions were theoretical rather than practical in these matters.

### On his reason for making a commercial for American Express

To pay for my American Express

# Likes

I like to give occasional parties, especially in Paris. Our last one went on to four o'clock in the morning but we had no complaints. Just three letters from total strangers saying how much they'd enjoyed an enchanting evening!

I like press interviews. They force one to crystallize one's flood of thought.

I do enjoy food, but I cook nightmarishly. The only time I lose weight is when I cook for myself and it is so nauseating that I keep thinking, 'Oh well, I'll wait for the next meal.'

### On his own jokes (at a party)

I don't laugh at my own jokes unless they're very good. That one was particularly good.

# *Dislikes*

I hate the thought of resting on my laurels. Laurels can come to feel very much like holly.

Two forms of animal life that I dislike intensely are lip-readers and people who pose a question but can't wait for a reply. I think most of the latter breed become television interviewers.

## On bores

I find that a most effective way of quelling bores is simply to say, suddenly and irrelevantly 'Now, Singapore – does that mean anything to you?

## On producing

I don't like ambitious films anymore. I don't like the fact that you have five and a half million dollars breathing down your neck the whole time.

## On the army

I believe that generals detest generals on their own side far more than they dislike the enemy.

I VERY MUCH DISLIKE PEOPLE
WHO PICK THEIR TEETH WITH
A COVERING HAND

I very much dislike people who pick their teeth with a covering hand.

## On clichés

Clichés are highly horrible things, but truths must be said. In the end you find that all clichés are true – and that's the bitterest pill of all.

## On suburban civilization

Suburban civilization makes grim demands. Caravanners travel miles to set up their tents in accurate rows in camping preserves which supply the comforts of nomadic life from well-stocked kiosks. I can understand the call of the wild – the call of the car-park is a little more esoteric.

## On official dress

Why do people dress up for formal occasions? I find the launching of battleships, or something like that, an irresistibly comic spectacle. Why do people have to put on hats with feathers blowing in the wind? I see no difference really between that and tribal garb in the African jungle.

## On being sensible

To be mild, to be tolerant, to be wise and sensible – you've got to be really tough.

# *Men, Women and Children*

## ON CHILDREN

There is a cliché which maintains that traits of character tend to jump one generation, and if such is in fact the case, it is probably due to a tendency of children to react against their parents in their formative years rather than to any purely genetic reasons.

### On what attracts him most about women

When a man's attracted to a woman all rules go out of the window.

### On mankind

The main difference between man and animal is man's ability to laugh.

### On his children

It suited our purpose admirably to stay in Hollywood a little longer, since Suzanne was reaching the term of her pregnancy, and she could not travel any more. She has been to a celebrated paediatrician whose only interest seemed to be the extent of my salary, since, he explained, he took one-tenth of it, which was deductible in my case. I began to have nightmares about being chided by the tax-man for not having had twins, so that one of them could be put down to business, and leave the other for pleasure.

THE MAIN DIFFERENCE BETWEEN MAN AND ANIMAL IS MAN'S ABILITY TO LAUGH

## On children

When you're very old you know that children have the right idea. If only they had the authority.

## On moments of assessment

The birth of each child registers the fact that nothing will ever be quite the same again. There is a new element to consider, a new character will be forming in the shelter of the nest in order eventually to join in the struggle for survival, armed I hope, and hoped, with a few parental virtues, and unhindered by too many parental vices.

## On missing out on history

When I was born my own grandmother was forty-five – no more than middle-aged and with years ahead to give her grandchildren. Over the weekend, we saw a woman of fifty-three displaying her 'miracle baby'. It should have been a picture of a proud granny, not a new mum. Profoundly unnatural, it gave you a glimpse of a future where grandparents will be a thing of the past. And where children will be denied a piece of their history.

## ON GRANDPARENTS

Parents are the bones on which children sharpen their teeth. Grandparents have a different role altogether: they provide the forbidden fruits (sherbet lemons in my case) on which children *break* their teeth. Parents invariably disappoint their children, seldom fulfilling the promise of their early years. Not grandparents: they are fully formed by the time you get to know them and, with luck, remain a loving constant. While parents fret about exam results and personal hygiene, the best grandparents offer a wonderful sense of acceptance. It seems enough for them that you are alive and well.

## ON CHILDREN

Watching children grow up is a great delight. You see in them your own faults and your wife's virtues, and that can be a very stabilizing influence.

MEMORY, THEY SAY,
PLAYS TRICKS